www.providencebooks.net

Publisher Contact

Email:contact@providencebooks.net

Social media: facebook.com/providencebooks

Acknowledgements

The team at Providence Books would like to thank our friends, family, suppliers and customers for making our vision of creating the highest-quality books a reality. Thanks for purchasing and enjoy the quotes!

This page is intentionally left blank

This page is intentionally left blank

Acting helped me as I was growing up. It helped me learn about myself, helped me travel, helped me understand life, express myself, all those wonderful things. So I'm very, very grateful; it's a fun job. It's a luxury.

Angelina Jolie

All women do have a different sense of sexuality, or sense of fun, or sense of like what's sexy or cool or tough.

Angelina Jolie

Anytime I feel lost, I pull out a map and stare. I stare until I have reminded myself that life is a giant adventure, so much to do, to see.

Angelina Jolie

Brad and I have never wanted our kids to be actors, but we also want them to be around film and be a part of Mommy and Daddy's life and for it not to be kept from them, either. We just want them to have a good, healthy relationship with it.

Angelina Jolie

Breast cancer alone kills some 458,000 people each year, according to the World Health Organization, mainly in low- and middle-income countries. It has got to be a priority to ensure that more women can access gene testing and lifesaving preventive treatment, whatever their means and background, wherever they live.

Angelina Jolie

Everyone got kind of crazy with me mentioning I was in love with a woman.

Angelina Jolie

First and foremost comes my family and my life with Brad. We have so much joy in raising our children and teaching them about the world that nothing really compares to that.

Angelina Jolie

Homework's hard. Especially math. My kids joke with me. They tell me they have homework. I say, 'Okay.' And then I sit down and they say, 'It's math.' 'No! Not math! English, history, anything!'

Angelina Jolie

Honestly, I like everything, boyish girls, girlish boys, the heavy and the skinny.

Angelina Jolie

I always felt caged, closed in, like I was punching at things that weren't there. I always had too much energy for the room I was in.

Angelina Jolie

I always play women I would date.

Angelina Jolie

I always wanted a great love affair: something that feels big and full, really honest, and enough. No moment should feel slight, false, or a little off. For me, it had to be everything.

Angelina Jolie

I am a strong believer that without justice, there is no peace. No lasting peace, anyway.

Angelina Jolie

I am deeply grateful to the citizens of Sarajevo and the Sarajevo Canton assembly for bestowing upon me this incredible honor of citizenship. I am so proud to now be a part of such an extraordinary part of the world and fellow citizen to the people I deeply love and admire.

Angelina Jolie

I am odd-looking. I sometimes think I look like a funny Muppet.

Angelina Jolie

I became an actress because my mom wanted me to become an actress. It took me until my mid-30s to realize I actually didn't. I actually wanted to write and direct and be more involved in politics and humanitarian issues.

Angelina Jolie

I didn't die young. So I am very lucky. There are other artists and people that didn't survive certain things... people can imagine that I did the most dangerous, and I did the worst... for many reasons, I shouldn't be here.

Angelina Jolie

I didn't really want to live, so anything that was an investment in time made me angry... but also I just felt sad. When the hopelessness is hurting you, it's the fixtures and fittings that finish you off.

Angelina Jolie

I do have tatoos, and I do wear leather, but there are other sides of me, that my film express.

Angelina Jolie

I don't believe in guilt; I believe in living on impulse as long as you never intentionally hurt another person. And don't judge people in your life. I think you should live completely free.

Angelina Jolie

I don't see myself as beautiful, because I can see a lot of flaws. People have really odd opinions. They tell me I'm skinny, as if that's supposed to make me happy.

Angelina Jolie

I don't see the point of doing an interview unless you're going to share the things you learn in life and the mistakes you make. So to admit that I'm extremely human and have done some dark things I don't think makes me unusual or unusually dark. I think it actually is the right thing to do, and I'd like to think it's the nice thing to do.

Angelina Jolie

I don't think the money people in Hollywood have ever thought I was normal, but I am dedicated to my work and that's what counts.

Angelina Jolie

I get impatient with people working on a film that have their head in their hands like it's the most complicated thing in the world.

Angelina Jolie

I grew up as this very carefree, happy kid then things turned darker for me. Maybe it was because I saw that the world wasn't as happy a place as I had hoped it would be for me.

Angelina Jolie

I had a C-section, and I found it fascinating. I didn't find it a sacrifice, and I didn't find it a painful experience. I found it a fascinating miracle of what a body can do.

Angelina Jolie

I have so much in my life. I want to be of value to the world.

Angelina Jolie

I learned to fly a few years ago in England. It's the only place I'm completely alone - up in the air, detached from everything.

Angelina Jolie

I like everything. Boyish girls, girlish boys, the heavy and the skinny. Which is a problem when I'm walking down the street.

Angelina Jolie

I like someone who is a little crazy but coming from a good place. I think scars are sexy because it means you made a mistake that led to a mess.

Angelina Jolie

I like to hide behind the characters I play. Despite the public perception, I am a very private person who has a hard time with the fame thing.

Angelina Jolie

I love great journalism. I appreciate it. I love a good, you know, I love good news stories. I love great books. I love great articles. I appreciate them so much, and they've been part of my education as a woman.

Angelina Jolie

I love to put on lotion. Sometimes I'll watch TV and go into a lotion trance for an hour. I try to find brands that don't taste bad in case anyone wants to taste me.

Angelina Jolie

I loved being Maleficent. I was quite sad to put my staff down and put my horns away because somehow, she just lives in a different world.

Angelina Jolie

I need more sex, OK? Before I die I wanna taste everyone in the world.

Angelina Jolie

I never felt settled or calm. You can't really commit to life when you feel that.

Angelina Jolie

I never like being touched, ever. People used to say I held my breath when they were hugging me. I still do.

Angelina Jolie

I never thought I'd have children; I never thought I'd be in love, I never thought I'd meet the right person. Having come from a broken home - you kind of accept that certain things feel like a fairy tale, and you just don't look for them.

Angelina Jolie

I notice that my characters go out to dinner and have fun and take these great trips, but I spend so much time on their lives, I don't have much of a personal life of my own. I have to sort of remember to fill out that little notebook on me.

Angelina Jolie

I seem to be getting a lot of things pushed my way that are strong women. It's like people see Hackers and they send me offers to play tough women with guns, the kind who wear no bra and a little tank top. I'd like to play strong women who are also very feminine.

Angelina Jolie

I take my kids to school. And if I go to work, I go to work, and they visit me on set. I come home. I have dinner with my family. I have breakfast with my family. I have a very solid, very warm home.

Angelina Jolie

I think I should learn French and be a better cook - basic, really good life stuff.

Angelina Jolie

I think all women go through periods where we hate this about ourselves, we don't like that. It's great to get to a place where you dismiss anything you're worried about. I find flaws attractive. I find scars attractive.

Angelina Jolie

I think if you make a good movie, people walk away arguing.

Angelina Jolie

I think the depth, what children can handle and what they're interested in, is much deeper than I think what people assume. I think it's why sometimes we make things too simple for them.

Angelina Jolie

I want to work; then, as my kids get older, I want to have adventures. I want to visit all their countries: learn and live inside all their cultures.

Angelina Jolie

I was of the generation where most of the Disney princesses and female characters were not girls that I admired. They just weren't characters I looked up to and identified with.

Angelina Jolie

I was the punk outsider who nobody messed with. I was fearless. At 16, I graduated and moved out.

Angelina Jolie

I went through a period when I felt my film characters were having more fun than I was. It might partly explain why I ended up tattooed or doing certain extreme things in my life.

Angelina Jolie

I'd go from film to film and almost detach from one world and jump in another. I was living as these people and not having a self. I didn't know who I was. And things just get really dark.

Angelina Jolie

I'd like to believe that the people that have supported me in my work or identified with me in films, the people that feel they know me, they do and they don't have misconceptions - they understand. I believe that.

Angelina Jolie

I'm a woman, and anytime you tell a woman that she looks nice, it's not going to upset her.

Angelina Jolie

I'm always doing something. I never shut my brain off. I always have something going on.

Angelina Jolie

I'm getting a wrinkle above my eyebrow because I just can't stop lifting it, and I love that you know.

Angelina Jolie

I'm happy being myself, which I've never been before. I always hid in other people, or tried to find myself through the characters, or live out their lives, but I didn't have those things in mine.

Angelina Jolie

I'm just glad I was able to return to some of that innocence and beauty I had as a child when I started my own family, and my children brought me back some of that spirit.

Angelina Jolie

I'm not somebody that just wants to hold up a white flag and say, 'Let's all just get along.' I think people that do horrible things should be held accountable.

Angelina Jolie

I'm not somebody that thinks about destiny and fate, but I don't walk away from it when something unfolds.

Angelina Jolie

I'm odd looking. Sometimes I think I look like a funny muppet.

Angelina Jolie

I'm terrible at reading scripts. I love to read, and I hate reading scripts.

Angelina Jolie

I've been reckless, but I'm not a rebel without a cause.

Angelina Jolie

I've learned that we all change constantly. It's rare to find that person who is growing with you in the same way at the same time, who encourages you to grow.

Angelina Jolie

I've never lived my life in the opinion of others. I believe I'm a good person. I believe I'm a good mom. But that's for my kids to decide, not for the world.

Angelina Jolie

I've realized that being happy is a choice. You never want to rub anybody the wrong way or not be fun to be around, but you have to be happy. When I get logical and I don't trust my instincts - Thats when I get in trouble.

Angelina Jolie

I've told Billy if I ever caught him cheating, I wouldn't kill him because I love his children and they need a dad. But I would beat him up. I know where all of his sports injuries are.

Angelina Jolie

If I didn't have my films as an outlet for all the different sides of me, I would probably be locked up.

Angelina Jolie

If I make a fool of myself, who cares? I'm not frightened by anyone's perception of me.

Angelina Jolie

If I think more about death than some other people, it is probably because I love life more than they do.

Angelina Jolie

If every choice you make comes from an honest place, you're solid, and nothing anybody can say about you can rock you or change your opinion.

Angelina Jolie

If you ask people what they've always wanted to do, most people haven't done it. That breaks my heart.

Angelina Jolie

If you don't get out of the box you've been raised in, you won't understand how much bigger the world is.

Angelina Jolie

If you have enough people sitting around telling you you're wonderful, then you start believing you're fabulous, then someone tells you you stink and you believe that too!

Angelina Jolie

In my father's generation, the product was 80 percent of what you were putting into the world, and your personal life was 20 percent. It now seems that 80 percent of the product I put out is silly, made-up stories and what I'm wearing.

Angelina Jolie

It was weird to be married; you kind of lose your identity. You're suddenly somebody's wife. And you're like, 'Oh, I'm half of a couple now. I've lost me.'

Angelina Jolie

It's a great thing about being pregnant - you don't need excuses to pee or to eat.

Angelina Jolie

It's getting harder to make decisions to just want to do something to work... I'm trying to find things that are extremely challenging or mean something to me deeply.

Angelina Jolie

It's hard to be clear about who you are when you are carrying around a bunch of baggage from the past. I've learned to let go and move more quickly into the next place.

Angelina Jolie

Life comes with many challenges. The ones that should not scare us are the ones we can take on and take control of.

Angelina Jolie

Like every parent, when you start your family, your life completely changes. And you completely live for someone else. I find that the most extraordinary thing. Your life is handed over to someone else. From that moment on, they come first in every choice you make. It's the most wonderful thing.

Angelina Jolie

Make bold choices and make mistakes. It's all those things that add up to the person you become.

Angelina Jolie

Maleficent has suffered abuse in the past, and there's a reason why she is now as furious as she is. And I think that children who have been outcast and abused in any way will relate to her. There's a beautiful side to her; she's not just a dark person. She has all these facets. And that is interesting.

Angelina Jolie

Maleficent was always so elegant. She always was in control. And to play her was difficult. I worked on my voice a lot. She's bigger than me. She's on a different level of performance that I have never done.

Angelina Jolie

My children love Maleficent's voice, so they always make me do it at home.

Angelina Jolie

My mother was a full-time mother. She didn't have much of her own career, her own life, her own experiences... everything was for her children. I will never be as good a mother as she was. She was just grace incarnate. She was the most generous, loving - she's better than me.

Angelina Jolie

Not many people know this about me, but I'm a natural blonde. My hair went from light blonde naturally to a darker kind of blonde. My mother dyed my hair dark when I was a child, as I loved the look then. So I'm basically a natural blonde.

Angelina Jolie

Obviously, there's a part of me that takes the world of violence and death very seriously. However, when it comes to protection, or when it comes to just the skill of shooting... I've gone to the range with sniper rifles and things like that.

Angelina Jolie

Oh, God, I struggle with low self-esteem all the time! I think everyone does. I have so much wrong with me, it's unbelievable!

Angelina Jolie

Once you have six children, you're committed.

Angelina Jolie

People wonder aloud about whether I am an okay mother. That is obviously painful because it's so important to me. It's hard to hear that people think I'm not a capable mother and a good person, that they just think I'm nuts.

Angelina Jolie

Real food, I've found, is actually better than dieting.

Angelina Jolie

Sadly, of course, there is real evil in the world. You watch the news, and you see all of the people suffering and so much cruelty.

Angelina Jolie

Sometimes I think my husband is so amazing that I don't know why he's with me. I don't know whether I'm good enough. But if I make him happy, then I'm everything I want to be.

Angelina Jolie

The fact is I am not having sex. But I feel absolutely ripe for the, what would you say? plucking?

Angelina Jolie

The great thing about having a bunch of kids is they just remind you that you're the person who takes them to go poop!

Angelina Jolie

The loss of a child is my greatest nightmare.

Angelina Jolie

The moment you have a child, in an instant your life is not for you, and your life is completely, 100 percent dedicated to another human being, and they will always come first. It changes you forever. It changes your perspective, and it gives you a nice purpose and focus.

Angelina Jolie

The side of fairytales I don't like is that they always have happy endings, that there's just good and evil, and things are perfect. But life is a little more complicated, and that's what I try to teach my kids.

Angelina Jolie

The truth is I love being alive. And I love feeling free. So if I can't have those things then I feel like a caged animal and I'd rather not be in a cage. I'd rather be dead. And it's real simple. And I think it's not that uncommon.

Angelina Jolie

Therapy? I don't need that. The roles that I choose are my therapy.

Angelina Jolie

There's certainly a side of me that isn't completely... sane. Or completely 'even' all the time. We all have our dark sides.

Angelina Jolie

There's nothing I have to hide or defend. I'm gonna live my life. And there are times when people wanna try to attack me, and I don't know why, but they will. And that's okay.

Angelina Jolie

There's people constantly asking you for something on set, so the multi-tasking of motherhood transfers very well to being a director. And I think you're compassionate.

Angelina Jolie

There's something about death that is comforting. The thought that you could die tomorrow frees you to appreciate your life now.

Angelina Jolie

They're right to think that about me, because I'm the person most likely to sleep with my female fans, I genuinely love other women. And I think they know that.

Angelina Jolie

To be in any way a positive contribution, that's all anybody wants to be. It's all I've ever wanted to be. I wanted to be an artist, be a mother. You want to feel that in your life you've been of use, in whatever way that comes out.

Angelina Jolie

To be intimate with a married man, when my own father cheated on my mother, is not something I could forgive. I could not look at myself in the morning if I did that. I wouldn't be attracted to a man who would cheat on his wife.

Angelina Jolie

War is so complex; human nature is so complex. There's no filmmaker who has ever figured it out perfectly.

Angelina Jolie

We have a choice about how we take what happens to us in our life and whether or not we allow it to turn us. We can become consumed by hate and darkness, or we're able to regain our humanity somehow, or come to terms with things and learn something about ourselves.

Angelina Jolie

What nourishes me also destroys me.

Angelina Jolie

When I first went to places where people were suffering from war and persecution, I felt ashamed of my feelings of sadness. I could see more possibilities in my life.

Angelina Jolie

When I get logical, and I don't trust my instincts - that's when I get in trouble.

Angelina Jolie

When I was growing up, I wanted to adopt, because I was aware there were kids that didn't have parents.

Angelina Jolie

When I was little... I didn't relate to princesses. I saw Maleficent, and I just thought she was so - she was so elegant.

Angelina Jolie

When other little girls wanted to be ballet dancers I kind of wanted to be a vampire.

Angelina Jolie

When you are an actor, you have to stay inside this world, but when you are with the crew, on the outside, you are in the dirt, working through all the issues. It's just a different way of working, and I think I preferred it.

Angelina Jolie

Where ever I am I always find myself looking out the window wishing I was somewhere else.

Angelina Jolie

Without pain, there would be no suffering, without suffering we would never learn from our mistakes. To make it right, pain and suffering is the key to all windows, without it, there is no way of life.

Angelina Jolie

Women have a certain sexuality, and I think their bodies are beautiful, and I'm not embarrassed to explore that in a film. But there are things you get offered that are vulgar and violent - just like there's a side of me that's vulgar and violent.

Angelina Jolie

This page is intentionally left blank

This page is intentionally left blank

This page is intentionally left blank

This page is intentionally left blank

This page is intentionally left blank